THE 26 TRADITIONAL AMERICAN DRUMMING RUDIMENTS

WITH ROLL CHARTS & RUDIMENTAL DRUM SOLOS

ISBN 978-1-4234-6431-0

HAL•LEONARD®
CORPORATION
7777 W. BLUEMOUND RD. P.O. BOX 13819 MILWAUKEE, WI 53213

In Australia Contact:
Hal Leonard Australia Pty. Ltd.
4 Lentara Court
Cheltenham, Victoria, 3192 Australia
Email: ausadmin@halleonard.com.au

Copyright © 1960 by John S. Pratt
All Rights Reserved
No part of this publication may be reproduced in any form
or by any means without the prior written permission of the Publisher.

Visit Hal Leonard Online at
www.halleonard.com

FOREWORD

The year of 2009 marks the fiftieth anniversary of the very first published works by now legendary percussion composer John S. Pratt. To celebrate this mark, Hal Leonard Corporation is very pleased to re-issue *The 26 Traditional American Drumming Rudiments*, along with several forthcoming works by Mr. Pratt. I am very excited that Hal Leonard is making these materials, with new prefaces and corrected music, available once again.

John (Jack) S. Pratt, U.S. Army retired, is one of America's greatest rudimentalists, percussion composers, and finest gentlemen. Now internationally known for his compositions, teaching, and historic performances, Jack was the instructor of the U.S. Military Academy Band "Hellcats" drum line at West Point. Jack was also an instructor of the Hawthorne Caballeros drum and bugle corps drum line, which won four DCA World Championships and three American Legion National Championships under his direction. Jack founded the International Association of Traditional Drummers (I.A.T.D.) in 2004, which recognizes rudimental drumming excellence, and promotes and preserves the "Traditional" drumming art form. He was inducted into the World Drum Corps Hall of Fame, American Patriots Rudimental Drummers Club Hall of Fame, the Percussive Arts Society Hall of Fame, and the New Jersey Drum and Bugle Corps Hall of Fame. Jack deserves honor and recognition for his life-long commitment to rudimental drumming excellence and for his enthusiasm in passing on the art of "Traditional" Rudimental Drumming. I anticipate that *The 26 Traditional American Drumming Rudiments* will reinvigorate your study of "Traditional" Rudimental Drumming and provide material for your drum line, marching bands, percussionists, library, and/or general drumming pleasure.

Ben Hans
January 2009

CONTENTS

Preface	3
Part I (A) The 26 Traditional American Drum Rudiments and Their Variations	4
The Long Roll	4
The Five Stroke Roll	4
The Seven Stroke Roll	4
The Flam	5
The Flam Accent	5
The Flam Paradiddle	5
The Flamacue	5
The Ruff	6
The Single Drag	6
The Double Drag	6
The Double Paradiddle	6
The Single Ratamacue	7
The Triple Ratamacue	7
The Single Stroke Roll	8
The Nine Stroke Roll	9
The Ten Stroke Roll	10
The Eleven Stroke Roll	10
The Thirteen Stroke Roll	11
The Fifteen Stroke Roll	11
The Flam Tap	12
The Single Paradiddle	12
The Drag Paradiddle No. 1	12
The Drag Paradiddle No. 2	12
The Flam Paradiddle-Diddle	13
The Lesson 25	13
The Double Ratamacue	13
Part I (B) Rudimental Roll Comparison Charts	14
Table A in 2/4 Time	14
Table B in 2/4 Time	15
Table C in 6/8 Time	16
Table D in 6/8 Time	17
Additional Ways of Notating Rudimental Rolls	18
Part II: Rudimental Drum Solos	19
The Sons of Liberty	20
(Contains the 13 Essential Rudiments)	
The All-American Emblem	22
(Contains all of the 26 Traditional American Drum Rudiments)	

PREFACE

I have long been engaged in a crusade to resurrect the 26 Standard American Drum Rudiments, which have been largely ignored since the breakup of the National Association of Rudimental Drummers (N.A.R.D.) in the late 1970s, or—if noticed—the "Traditional" rudiments have been added to and have had some of their basic rhythms altered and their "Traditional" names changed. This is an insult that could only be compared to people deciding to add stars to the Colonial American flag that represented the 13 original colonies of the United States. Thank God that it never happened.

In any case, through the years since 1776, America's "Traditional" spirit has slowly declined. Since the American Revolution, the drumming books of Charles Ashworth (1812), Bruce and Emmett (1862), and Gardner Strube (1869) helped to sustain what finally were drawn together as the 26 Standard American Drum Rudiments, which were approved by the U.S. Government as part of the officially recognized Camp Duty. Late in 1933, a group of 13 drummers, which included J. Burns Moore, George Lawrence Stone, and William F. Ludwig, Sr., gathered together at an American Legion National Convention held in Chicago and put the final touches on the American Rudimental Drumming System by forming the N.A.R.D. They established a group of "13 Essential Rudiments" and 13 additional rudiments to make a total of 26. I have often thought that the 13 men who formed the N.A.R.D. may have chosen two sets of 13 rudiments to honor the 13-star American Colonial flag and the "Spirit of 1776" that the Colonial flag represented.

Why anyone, or any group, would ever regard the 26 Standard American Drum Rudiments as a subject for change is beyond belief, but in recent years, groups of individuals have chosen to expand the "Tradition" by adding to it, renaming the ruff as a drag and changing the rhythms of the original single and double drags. They have also added a number of rhythmic configurations from the Swiss "Traditional" drumming system and other "new" rhythmic patterns. This so-called "International" list has now exceeded 40 in number. But, since "Tradition" has its roots in history, it cannot be modified, added to, or mingled with the "Traditional" drumming forms of other countries. Every country has developed its own drumming "Tradition," and their rhythmic configurations should never have been added to a list of so-called "International Rudiments." "Traditions" are grounded in history. If you change, alter, or add to "Traditions," you destroy history. Many American drummers have broken with their own "Tradition," which was firmly established in 1933 by the N.A.R.D. Other countries' drummers still follow their historic "Traditions," and so should we. Therefore, by forming in 2004 an International Association of "Traditional" Drummers (I.A.T.D.), I hoped to have united countries around the world, each with their own various forms and systems of "Traditional" drumming, and have renewed our own country's dedication to respecting our own "Traditional" system of the 26 Standard American Drum Rudiments.

John S. Pratt
Hawthorne, N.J.

PART I (A): THE 26 TRADITIONAL AMERICAN DRUM RUDIMENTS AND THEIR VARIATIONS

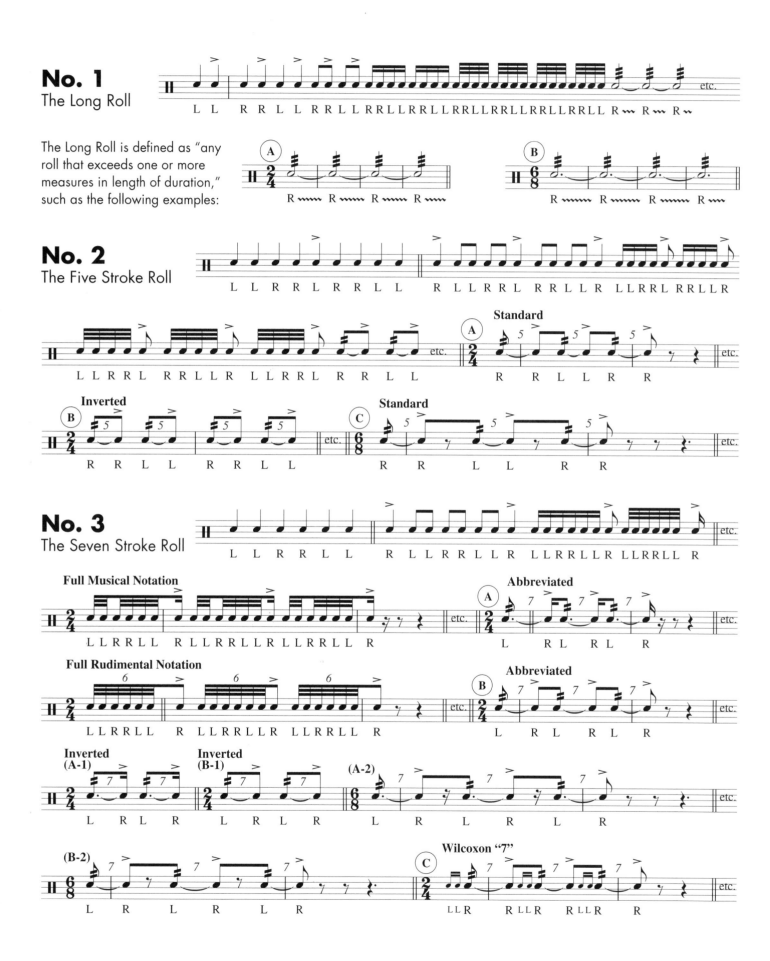

No. 1
The Long Roll

The Long Roll is defined as "any roll that exceeds one or more measures in length of duration," such as the following examples:

No. 2
The Five Stroke Roll

No. 3
The Seven Stroke Roll

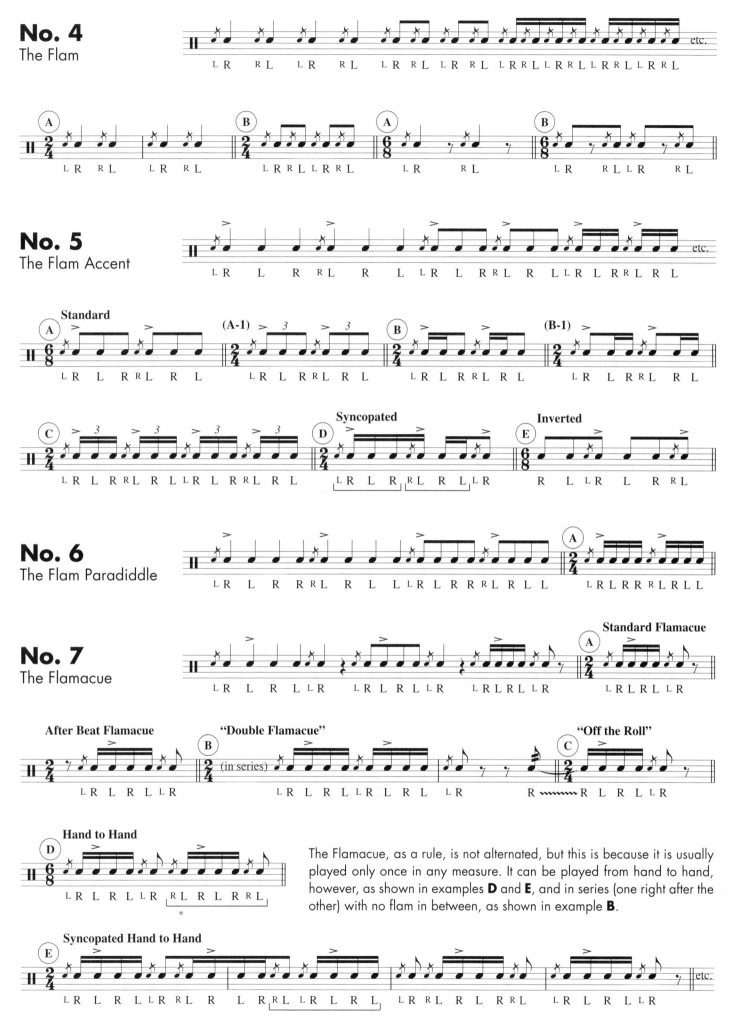

No. 4
The Flam

No. 5
The Flam Accent

No. 6
The Flam Paradiddle

No. 7
The Flamacue

The Flamacue, as a rule, is not alternated, but this is because it is usually played only once in any measure. It can be played from hand to hand, however, as shown in examples **D** and **E**, and in series (one right after the other) with no flam in between, as shown in example **B**.

*Indicates alternate or reverse sticking

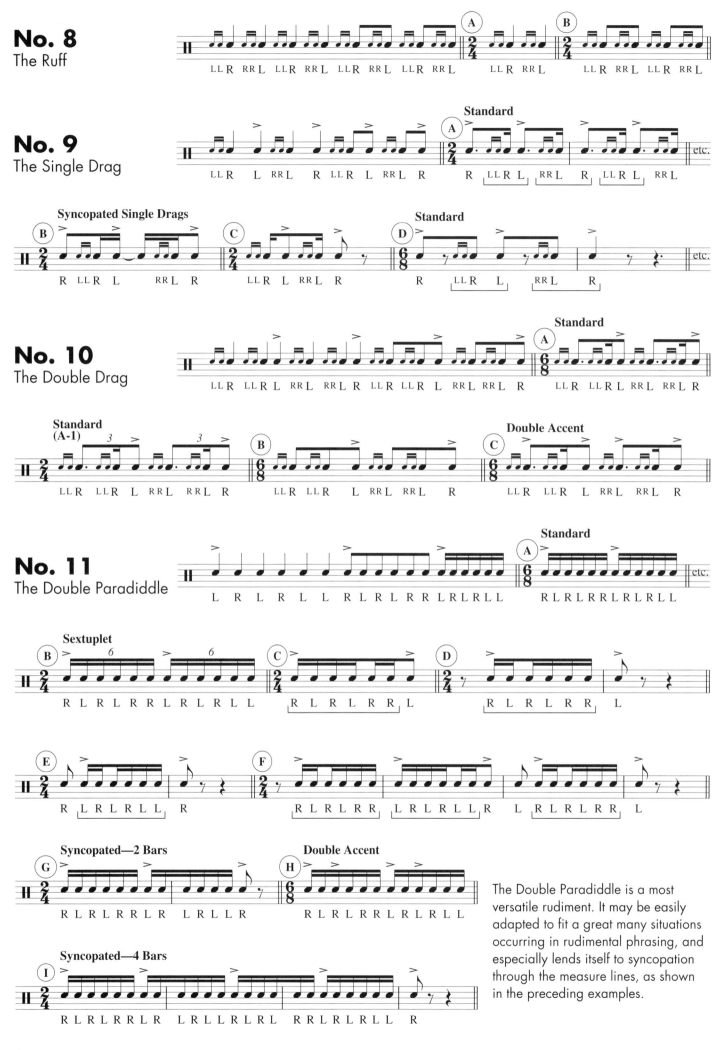

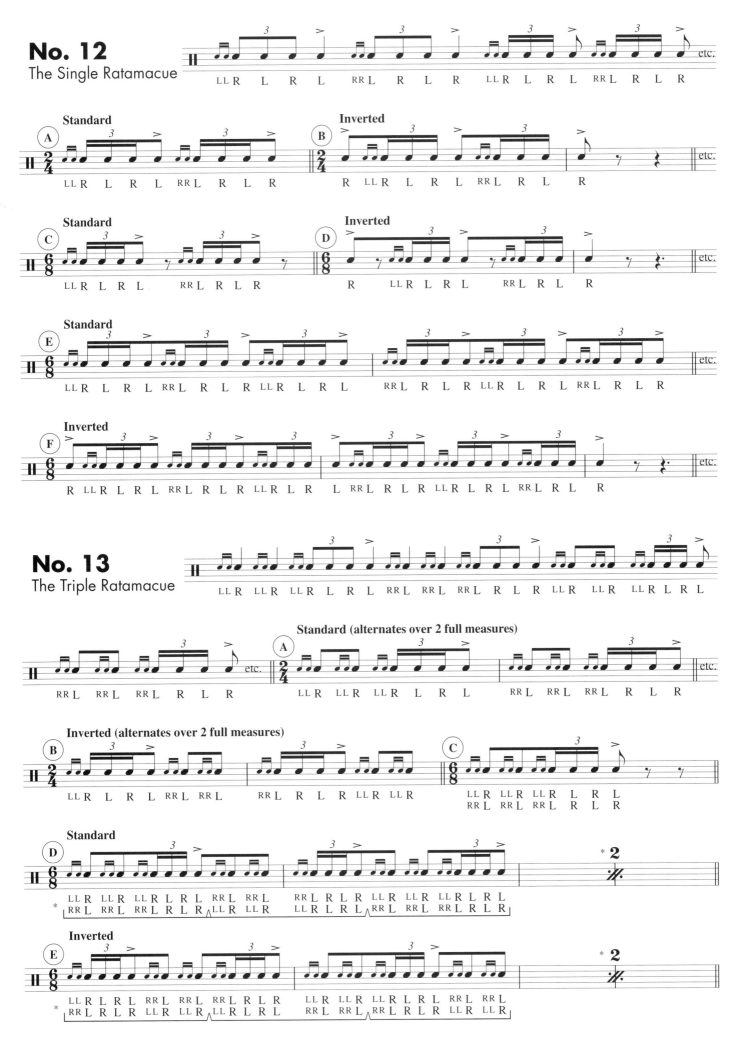

No. 12
The Single Ratamacue

No. 13
The Triple Ratamacue

*Alternate sticking on 2-bar repeat

No. 14
The Single Stroke Roll

The single stroke roll is divided into two main forms. The standard version (Example A) is more frequently used in Jazz or Dance drumming, while the triplet form is more common to Military drumming, such as is found in Drum and Bugle Corps, Marching Bands, or Fife and Drum units. The above examples (B through J) are the most widely used variations of the (triplet) single stroke roll, and are presented here for study and technical comparison.

† The 4 Stroke Ruff is employed to a great extent in concert work, where lightness of touch is needed to perform the many pianissimo passages, and where the regular Five Stroke Roll would be too coarse, even though played very closed.

No. 15
The Nine Stroke Roll

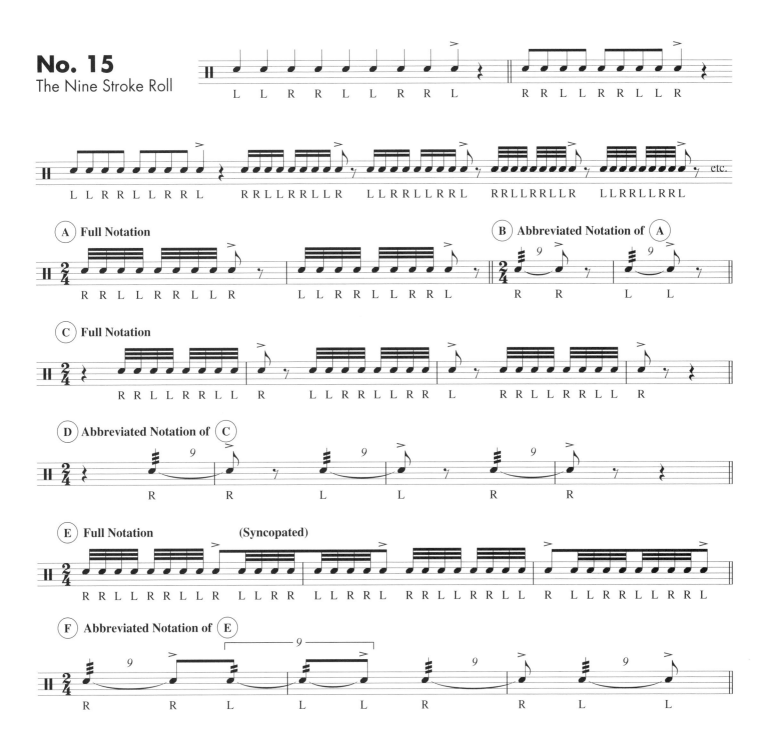

The Ten and Eleven Stroke Rolls, which immediately follow on the next page, need some explanation to place them in their proper light. First of all, they are rolls that are infrequently used, except in Drum and Bugle and Fife and Drum Corps, or in the rendition of ancient drum solos such as the "3 Camps," and as a rule are improperly notated when written in military 2/4's at 120 = ♩ time. Secondly, although the Eleven is a stroke longer than the Ten, they both require only *six* distinct hand motions to execute, and therefore the Ten is actually as long in length of duration as the Eleven. The Ten drops the last *two* 32nd notes (two lefts) in favor of *one* left 16th note, which gives the pronounced hop or double sound that so easily distinguishes the Ten from the Eleven.

The last point is that these rolls are both played "one way," from *left* to *right* only. They do not alternate when played one after the other in series, although it is entirely possible to start them on the right, in which case they must also end on that hand. The Ten and Eleven Stroke Rolls are technically difficult to execute properly and require concentrated study to perfect, but the mastering of such beats is a further aid in the development of a drummer's technique and all-around ability, and should not be dismissed lightly.

No. 16 †
The Ten Stroke Roll

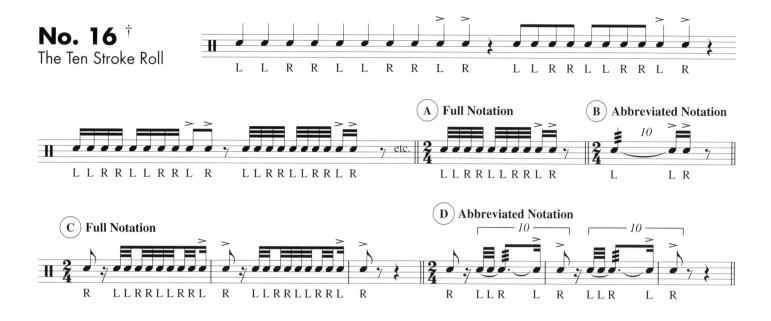

† This is perhaps the first time that the Ten Stroke Roll has been listed with a double accent, but it cannot be musically avoided. Due to a quirk of execution, even though little or no emphasis is placed on the ninth beat, it retains a slight accent, which is derived from the very nature of the Ten Stroke Roll's construction. The sudden change from 32nd notes to one 16th note, followed in quick succession by another accented note, will make the ninth beat stand out as if it were accented. This is contrary to long-established theories about notating this rudiment. However, from a musical standpoint, it is felt that any accent, implied or slight though it may be, should not be overlooked in the notation of any rudimental figure, and for this reason, the Ten Stroke Roll is listed here with two accents. This notation should more clearly establish the actual sound of this roll and aid in a more musical interpretation of it. Proper execution will be obtained, providing the first accent is played with just a bit less stress than the second accent.

No. 17
The Eleven Stroke Roll

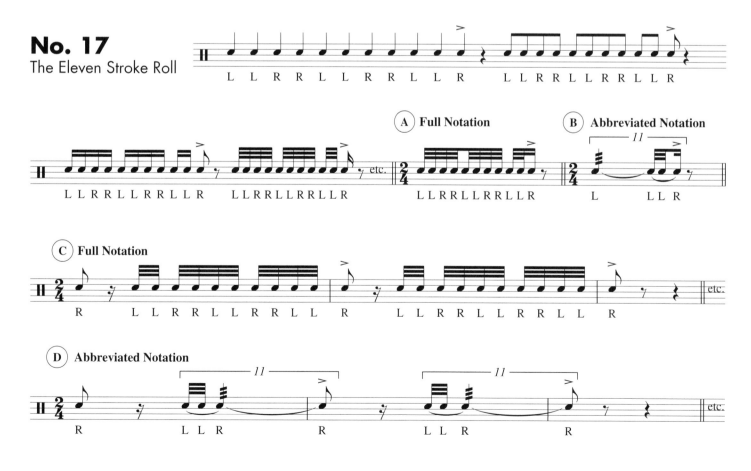

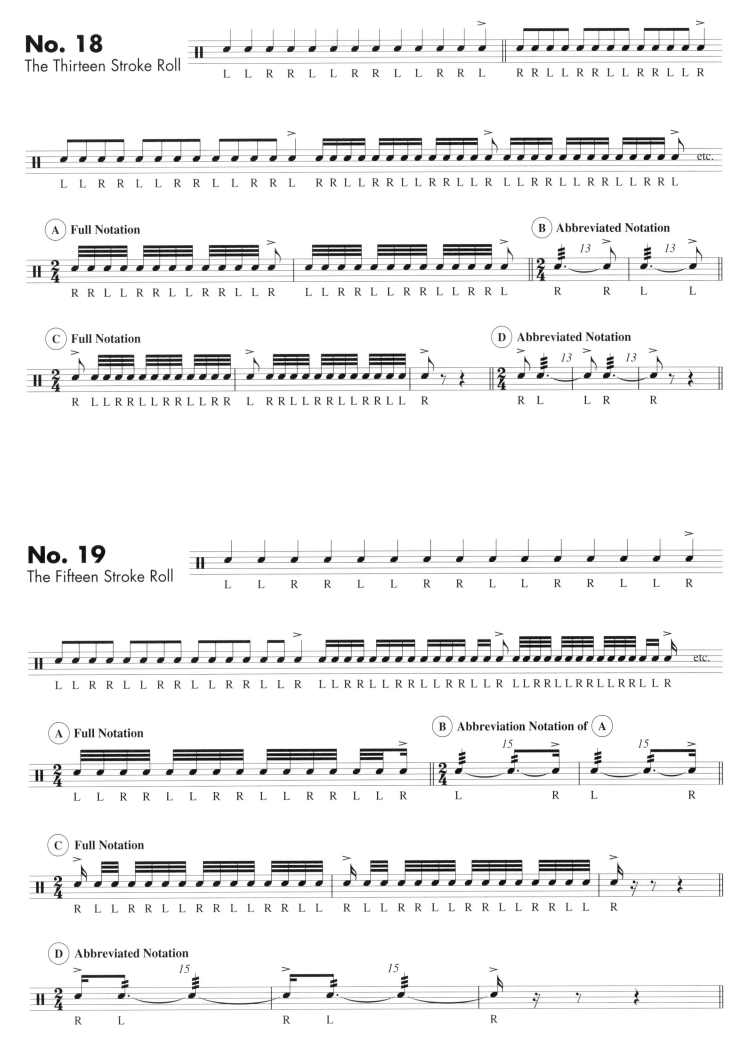

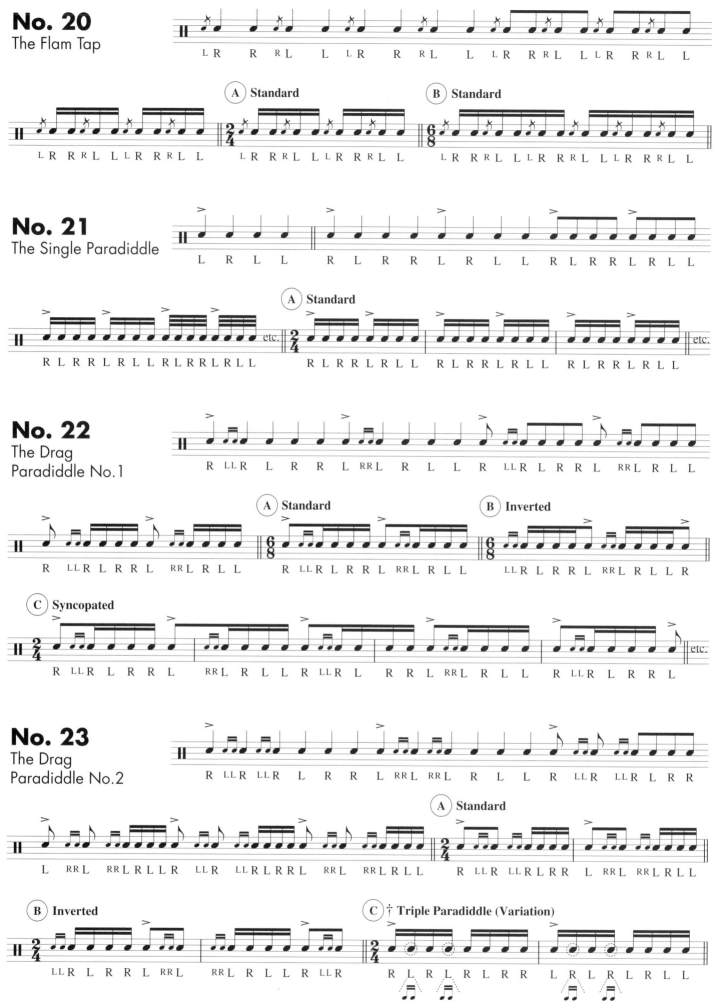

† When the grace notes are dropped and single 16th notes are substituted in their place, the variation, known as the Triple Paradiddle, is formed.

No. 24
The Flam
Paradiddle-Diddle

No. 25
The Lesson 25

No. 26
The Double Ratamacue

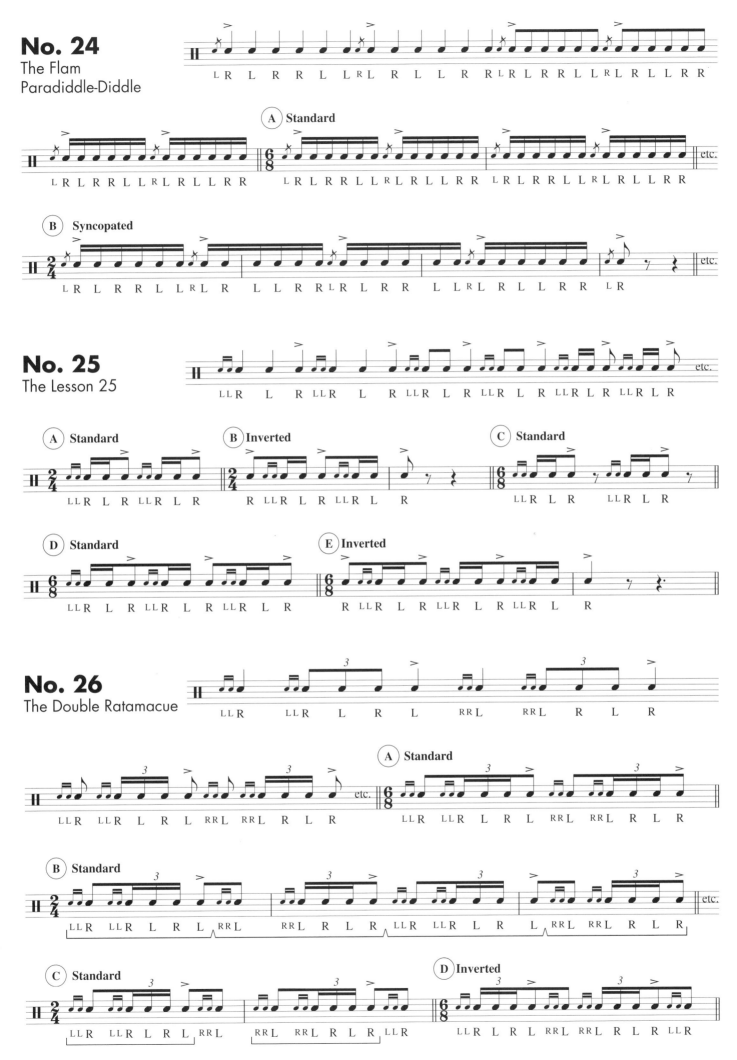

PART I (B): RUDIMENTAL ROLL COMPARISON CHARTS

The following table shows the exact note value of each of the short rudimental rolls by comparing them together on the basis of the long roll.

Table A deals with rudimental rolls **commencing** upon the measure.

Table A in 2/4 Time

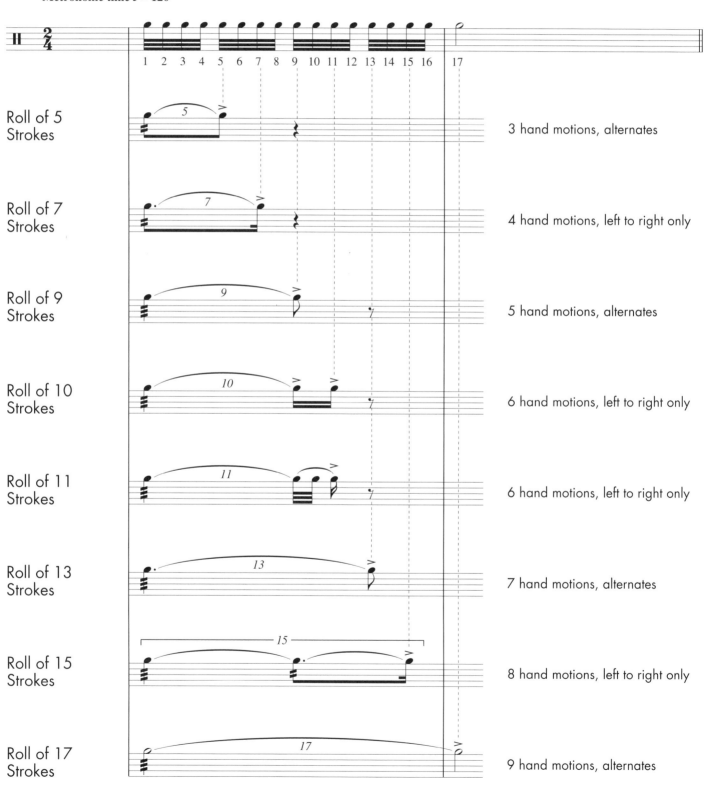

RUDIMENTAL ROLL COMPARISON CHART

The following table shows the exact note value of each of the short rudimental rolls by comparing them together on the basis of the long roll.

Table B deals with the rudimental rolls **ending** upon the measure.

Table B in 2/4 Time

Metronome time ♩ = 120

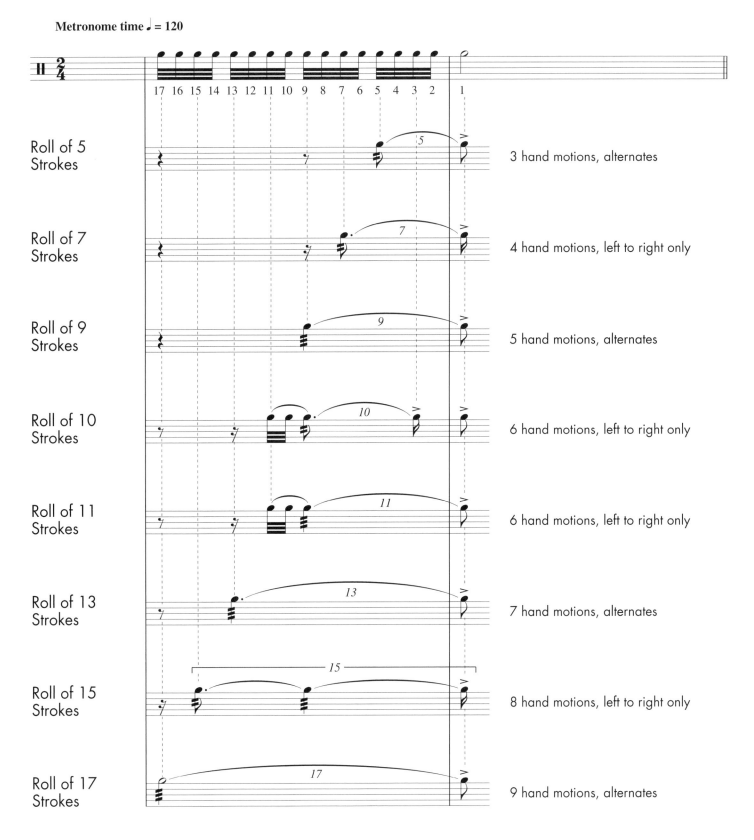

Rudimental Roll Comparisons in Slow 6/8

Table C deals with rudimental rolls **commencing** upon the measure.

Table C in 6/8 Time

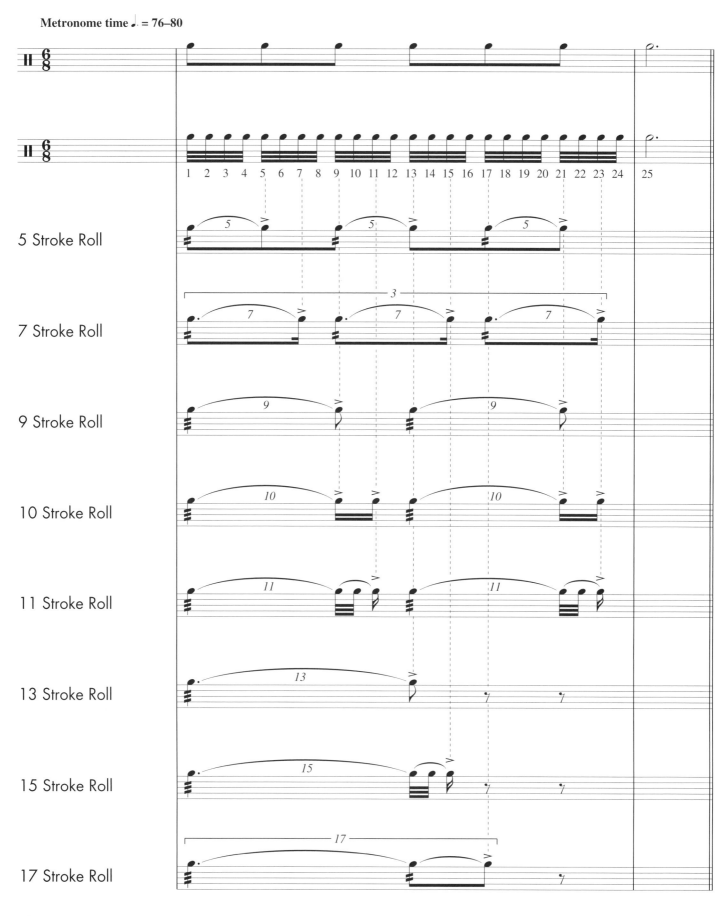

RUDIMENTAL ROLL COMPARISONS IN SLOW 6/8

Table D deals with rudimental rolls **commencing** upon the measure.

Table D in 6/8 Time

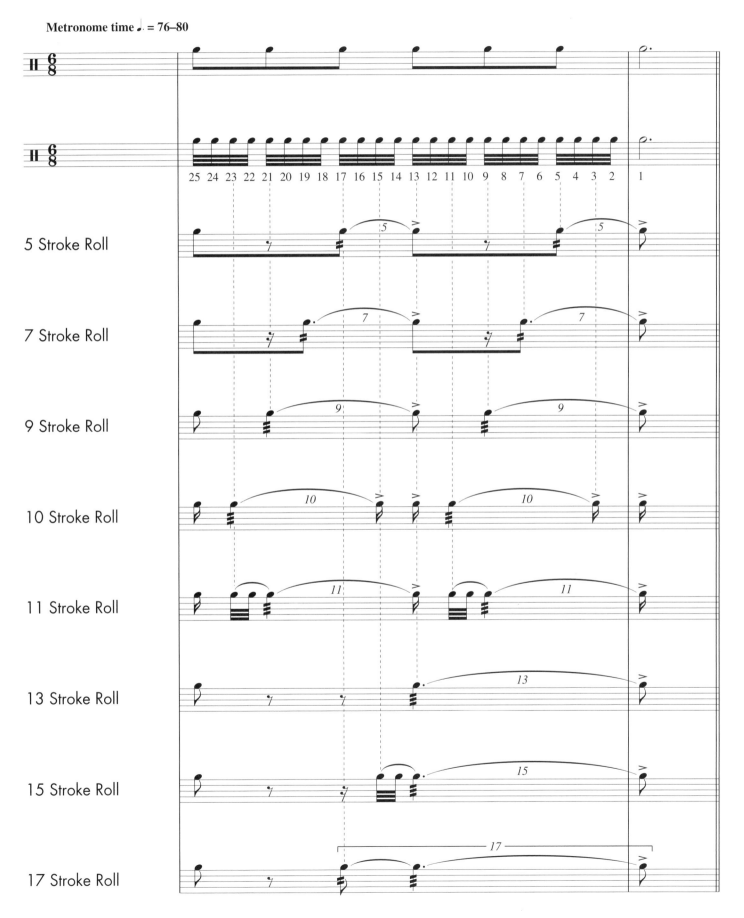

ADDITIONAL WAYS OF NOTATING RUDIMENTAL ROLLS

The rolls, as notated in the preceding comparison charts, were full musical notations based upon the indicated metronome tempos. However, depending upon how closed the drummer executes his rolls, the following possibilities also present themselves.

A seven can be played in the time of a five stroke roll.

A ten can be played in the time of a nine stroke roll.

An eleven can be played in the time of a nine stroke roll.

A fifteen can be played in the time of a thirteen stroke roll.

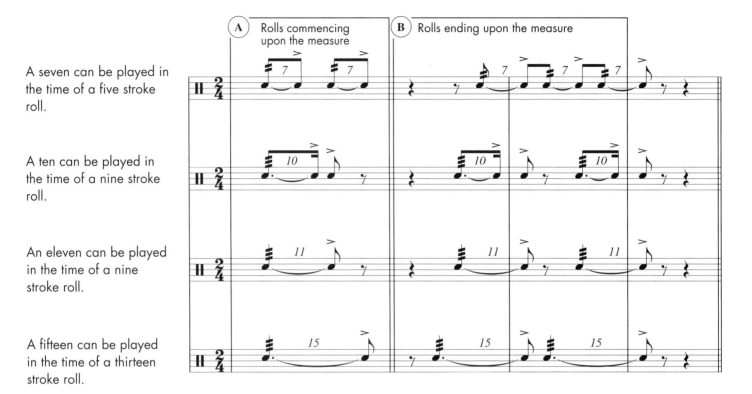

In fast 6/8 tempos, the rolls are sustained for the duration of the notation in accordance with the established tempo. The following examples indicate, as nearly as possible, the rudimental roll or rolls that can usually be applied to these notations at marching tempo, ♩.= 120.

Both **A** and **B** can be played as five or seven stroke rolls.

Both **A** and **B** can be played as nine or eleven stroke rolls.

A is usually played as a seventeen stroke roll.

B can be played as a thirteen or fifteen stroke roll.

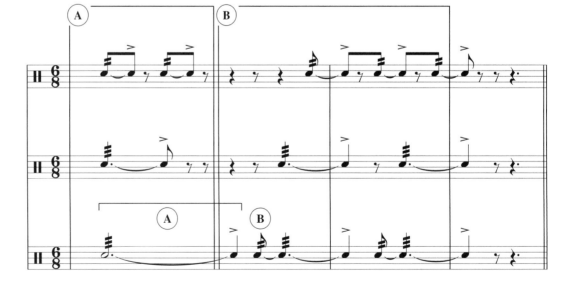

PART II

RUDIMENTAL DRUM SOLOS

On the following several pages, various rudiments have been applied in two drum solos in order to more clearly convey the manner in which rudiments can be utilized.

The first solo is entitled "The Sons of Liberty" and deals with the 13 Essential Rudiments, which for years have been the basic entrance examination requirements of the National Association of Rudimental Drummers.

The second solo is entitled "The All-American Emblem" and contains every one of the Traditional 26 American Drum Rudiments, all written in 2/4 time.

It is sincerely hoped that the mastery of these two solos will be an invaluable aid in the further understanding of the possibilities presented by the Rudimental System.

THE SONS OF LIBERTY

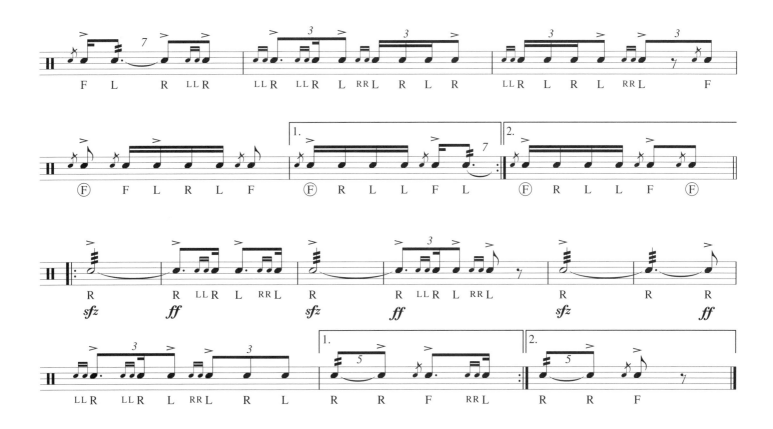

This solo contains the 13 Essential Rudiments of drumming as adopted by the National Association of Rudimental Drummers.

1. The Long Roll
2. The Five Stroke Roll
3. The Seven Stroke Roll
4. The Flam
5. The Flam Accent
6. The Flam Paradiddle

7. The Flamacue
8. The Ruff
9. The Single Drag
10. The Double Drag
11. The Double Paradiddle
12. The Single Ratamacue
13. The Triple Ratamacue

This solo is respectfully dedicated to the U.S. flag that represented the 13 original colonies in the Union.

A RUDIMENTAL DRUM SOLO FEATURING THE
26 TRADITIONAL AMERICAN RUDIMENTS

THE ALL-AMERICAN EMBLEM

Metronome time ♩ = 110

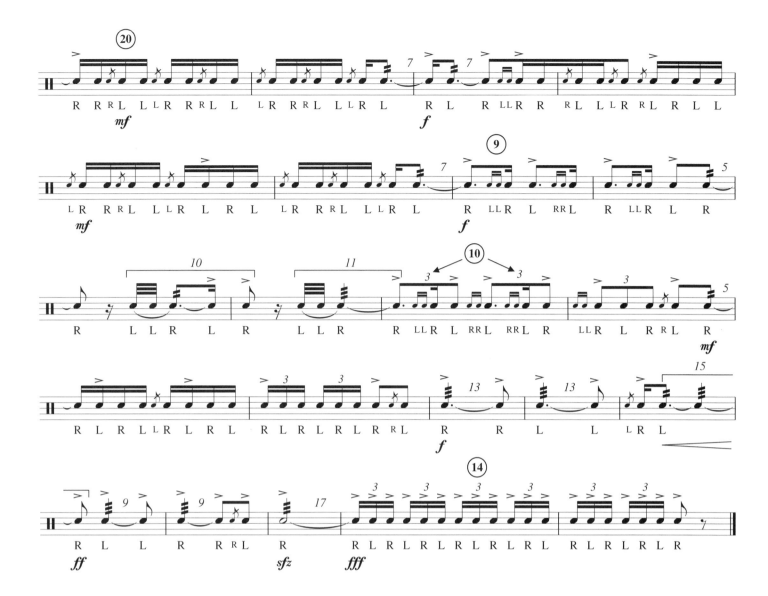

This solo contains the Standard 26 American Rudiments of drumming as adopted by the National Association of Rudimental Drummers.

1. The Long Roll
2. The Five Stroke Roll
3. The Seven Stroke Roll
4. The Flam
5. The Flam Accent
6. The Flam Paradiddle
7. The Flamacue
8. The Ruff
9. The Single Drag
10. The Double Drag
11. The Double Paradiddle
12. The Single Ratamacue
13. The Triple Ratamacue

14. The Single Stroke Roll
15. The Nine Stroke Roll
16. The Ten Stroke Roll
17. The Eleven Stroke Roll
18. The Thirteen Stroke Roll
19. The Fifteen Stroke Roll
20. The Flam Tap
21. The Single Paradiddle
22. The Drag Paradiddle No. 1
23. The Drag Paradiddle No. 2
24. The Flam Paradiddle-Diddle
25. The Lesson 25
26. The Double Ratamacue